THE WALLS

Colin Teevan
THE WALLS

OBERON BOOKS
LONDON

First published in 2001 by Oberon Books Ltd.
(incorporating Absolute Classics)
521 Caledonian Road, London N7 9RH
Tel: 020 7607 3637 / Fax: 020 7607 3629

e-mail: oberon.books@btinternet.com

A catalogue record for this book is available from the British Library.

ISBN: 1 84002 153 5

Cover photograph: Tom McShane

Author photograph: Pau Ros

Cover design: Humphrey Gudgeon

Series design: Richard Doust

Printed in Great Britain by Antony Rowe Ltd, Reading.

ACKNOWLEDGEMENTS

This play was workshopped at the Royal National Theatre Studio. The author would like to express his thanks and appreciation to Sue Higginson and Jack Bradley for their advice throughout the process. He also wishes to express his appreciation of the actors who took part in that workshop: Martin Savage, Frances Tomelty, Michael Culkin, Karl Johnson, JD Kellegher, Declan Conlon, Nina Conti, and Ciaran McIntyre; and finally the director then as now Mick Gordon.

for
Frank and Pauline

Characters

THE MAN

STELLA

THEO

TOM

JOHN

JOSEPH

MARY

SWEENEY

The Walls was first performed at the Royal National Theatre, (Cottesloe) on 9 March 2001, with the following cast:

THE MAN, Toby Jones

STELLA, Clare Higgins

THEO, Michael Culkin

TOM, Karl Johnson

JOHN, Gary Lydon

JOSEPH, Declan Conlon

MARY, Monica Dolan

SWEENEY, Tony Rohr

Director, Mick Gordon

Designer, Dick Bird

Lighting, Neil Austen

ACT ONE

A front room in a middle-class suburban house. There is a sofa, an armchair and a coffee table. Stage right a wall with a fireplace, mantelpiece with a family photograph on it, and a door that leads to a hall, stairs and the upstairs bedrooms; stage left a wall with a door that leads to the kitchen and, in the back wall, the hall door, a window, coat hooks and a Christmas tree.

It is evening, the room is in near darkness apart from a light that comes from the kitchen. The doorbell rings. STELLA enters. She turns on the main light, checks her watch, then goes to the door and opens it. There is a MAN with a toolbox.

MAN: Mrs Walls?

STELLA: O.

MAN: The Man from Oakwood.

STELLA: Yes, yes, of course.

MAN: Expecting someone else?

STELLA: My son. And his wife.

MAN: Well I suppose I'll have to do, for the moment.

STELLA: Yes, I suppose. I'd almost given up hope. Eight o'clock, Christmas Eve –

MAN: Ghost staff.

STELLA: Well, you'd best come in.

MAN: Understand. Can't be too careful.

The MAN comes downstage and puts his toolbox down.

MAN: Son coming for Christmas then?

STELLA: Yes.

MAN: Live far away?

STELLA: London.

MAN: O. Don't see him that often, then?

STELLA: Not in a number of years.

MAN: Must find that hard.

STELLA: Well –

MAN: Is she nice?

STELLA: Who?

MAN: Her.

STELLA: O, her. We've yet to meet.

MAN: Got a good job over there?

STELLA: He's in property. He has a degree.

MAN: Must be proud. Still, he should find the time to see his folks more often. He should appreciate what he's got. I love Christmas. Families and all that. Nice place you have here.

STELLA: Apart from the –

MAN: No worries, Mrs Walls. Soon have it set to rights.

MAN assesses the extent of the job.

STELLA: Will it be a big job, Mr – ?

MAN: Hard to tell at this stage. What's this that's out there?

STELLA: The park.

MAN: Must make for quite a vista. During the day.

STELLA: That's as may be, but we did not buy the house for access to the elements but protection from them.

MAN: Of course, Mrs Walls. Right. Let's get cracking. When did you first notice?

STELLA: This morning.

MAN: First thing?

STELLA: I came down for my All Bran –

MAN: Bit of a blockage?

STELLA: Please, I feel exposed enough as it is. Lord knows, there might be people out there – very nice people I'm sure – but people nevertheless – although I don't know what they expect to see and I'm sure they won't see whatever it is they do expect to see here – I just don't want to be on display like this, in my own living room –

MAN: I understand. So, how did you sleep last night, Mrs Walls?

STELLA: I beg your pardon?

MAN: Any noises?

STELLA: None.

MAN: A sound night's sleep, then?

STELLA: I wouldn't go that far.

MAN: O?

STELLA: Dreams. The dream. The usual dream.

MAN: The usual dream?

STELLA: I'm on a stage and there are people – I can't see them, but I know they're there, in the darkness, expecting something from me, some performance, only I don't know what I am to perform – Excuse me, but I took it to be an engineering problem?

MAN: Sorry Mrs Walls, didn't mean to pry. It's just that our dreams have a way of filtering reality, if you know what I mean. Any loud noises in this dream of yours then?

STELLA: No. In fact quite the contrary. A deathly silence.

MAN: And Mr Walls? Did he hear anything?

STELLA: He appeared oblivious. He usually appears that way.

MAN: Anyone else about?

STELLA: My son. My other son.

MAN: Where was he when this happened?

STELLA: In his room, I suppose.

MAN: Back for Christmas too?

STELLA: He has not been away to come back.

MAN: Just the two boys, then?

STELLA: Yes.

MAN: That must be nice. Never had a daughter?

STELLA: No.

MAN: You must have wanted one.

STELLA: Why do you say that?

MAN: Someone to pass the knowledge on to, I suppose. The
    mysteries of femininity. Like a man wants a son. I'm
    inclined to get a bit sentimental, when it comes to the
    family thing. I was brought up in a home.

STELLA: I'm sorry.

MAN: That's alright. Wasn't your fault, was it? Anyway, I'd
    best be getting on with it. And you'll have your sprouts
    to get back to.

STELLA: ?

MAN: The dinner. Tomorrow.

STELLA: Yes, I suppose –

MAN: While you're in there, you wouldn't be a love and put the kettle on?

STELLA disapprovingly assents and exits to kitchen. The MAN is about to take some measurements when he sees the framed photo on the mantelpiece. He looks at it briefly, then, making sure no one is watching, he puts the photo in his toolbox. He has just got back to his tools when THEO enters pushing TOM in a wheelchair. In the course of the following THEO manages to take off and hang up both his and TOM's coats etc.

TOM: – mark my words, Walls.

THEO: Don't doubt it, Tom –

TOM: The weight of the body on her means she's a whoor on the juice and a divil up a steep incline.

THEO: Best to avoid the heavy ones, eh?

TOM: You can't beat a Jap these days.

THEO: Indeed you can't, Tom.

MAN: Mr Walls?

THEO: Yes?

MAN: From Oakwood. I've come about the…the problem –

THEO: Of course. Theo Walls. It's the Man, Tom, from Oakwood. The developers. He's come at last –

TOM: Hallowed be his name.

MAN: Sorry about the delay. Busy time of the year. Seems like everyone's some problem needs fixing.

THEO: Better late than never. This is Tom, a neighbour –

TOM: *Dominus Vobiscum* –

THEO: He's a Jesuit. Used to teach in the school. These houses are built on the old playing fields. Oakwood paid three million –

TOM: Three and three quarter. Worth twice that now –

THEO: His sight is weak. I read the newspaper for him.

TOM: Is that the Man's VW outside?

MAN: What about it?

TOM: Tell him he'll regret it, Walls. Tell the Man he should have bought a Jap.

MAN: She does me.

TOM: Used to drive a Ford Zephyr myself. Black and shining chrome and red leather upholstery. She'd make the seat of your pants stick to your backside with the sweat on a hot day.

THEO: Was an Audi man myself. In my prime. Any ideas about the…the problem?

MAN: No fears, Mr Walls, I'll sort you out.

THEO: I hope so, though I can't help but feel that it will get worse before it gets better. That's been the way of things in the past.

TOM: And it won't do the value any favours, mark my words.

STELLA puts her head in. She is about to speak when she sees THEO and TOM.

STELLA: (*To MAN.*) I was going to ask you if you took milk and sugar, but I see we need more cups.

TOM: Great is Artemis of the Ephesians!

MAN: Milk and sugar would be grand, Mrs Walls.

THEO: I thought I'd ask him over Stella, being Christmas and all that. It can't be much fun for him there, on his own…

STELLA: I'd better open the mince pies.

THEO: He'd like that. You'd like that, wouldn't you, Tom?

TOM: Yes. Yes, I'd like that.

STELLA has returned to the kitchen.

THEO: I think she's a bit tense about the…you know.

MAN: Only natural.

THEO: Been with Oakwood long?

MAN: Since I qualified. Three years.

THEO: University?

MAN: Night courses. Used to be in waste.

THEO: Dirty business?

MAN: One blocked pipe and you're up to your tonsils in your family's shite. Pardon the language. Glad to leave the Corpo.

THEO: You were with the Corporation?

MAN: Since school.

THEO: You didn't know a Sweeney, in the Corpo?

MAN: No. Can't say I did.

THEO: Wonder what brought him to mind after all these years. Haven't come to him yet in my memoirs, Tom. I tell Tom about the old days. It helps him put down the day. Me and Sweeney did some work together back then. He got me planning permission for a factory. I had a company. Star of the Sea. Named the company after Stella. Latin for star. Stella Maris.

TOM: (*Singing.*) *'Stella Maris, Star of the Sea*
Pray for the wanderer, pray for me.'

MAN: Very romantic.

THEO: Made underpants. Very big. At one point. The business that is. We catered for all sizes.

MAN: Well, I can't say I've heard of your friend. No. Hang on. When I first worked there, there was talk of a Sweeney.

THEO: You see!

MAN: There was some story about him. He became a bit of a synonym.

THEO: For what?

MAN: For doing a Sweeney. I don't know, like I say he left before my time. I think there was something about the manner of his departure. Bit of a smell.

THEO: That will have been him alright.

STELLA enters from kitchen. She carries a tea-tray laden with cups, saucers etc. and a plate of mince pies.

STELLA: I hope Theo isn't distracting you?

MAN: Just telling me about an old mate of his.

STELLA: A mate? How interesting. How many sugars?

MAN: Two, cheers.

STELLA: Mince pie?

MAN: That's the business.

THEO: Sweeney. He got me planning for the Northside factory. Residents kicked up, but he pushed it through anyway.

STELLA: Tom? Your usual?

TOM: *Gratias tibi.*

THEO: You remember Sweeney, Stella? We saw quite a bit of him, at one point. Had him over to dinner on occasion.

STELLA: I really have no idea whom you are talking about, Theo. Tom, a mince pie?

TOM: Thank you.

THEO: You did that desert with the ginger snaps and the Cointreau and the cream.

TOM: Mmm. Excellent, Stella.

STELLA: Marks and Spencers.

TOM: The Jews, they could teach us a thing or two about Christmas –

JOHN enters from stage-right door to hall, stairs and landing. He ignores those present. He goes to the kitchen, returns with a mug, fills it and leaves by the door he entered. Pause.

MAN: Your other son?

STELLA: John, yes.

MAN: Lost in thought?

STELLA: That must be it.

JOHN re-enters from stage-right door, takes a mince pie and leaves by the door he entered. Pause.

THEO: I remember once we lost Joey as a child –

STELLA: I'm sure our guests aren't interested, Theo.

THEO: – Wicklow. '70 or '71. A caravan holiday by the sea. Off he trotted in his little red trunks –

STELLA: Can't it wait till later –

THEO: – and his net to fish for sprats in the rock pools.

STELLA: Why must you do this to me?

THEO: Only memories, dear. Only harmless memories. (*To TOM*.) Adventurous at that age. I'm sure I don't have to tell you anything about the adventurousness of young scamps, Tom.

TOM: No, Walls, you don't. I couldn't have another of those mince pies, Stella?

STELLA: So long as our other guest –

MAN: Don't mind me –

STELLA hands TOM a mince pie.

THEO: Didn't miss him till late afternoon. By then there was neither sight nor sound. In and out of rockpool I scrabbled –

STELLA: You must forgive me if I return to the kitchen.

MAN: The sprouts?

STELLA: To hell with the sprouts. I'm sorry.

STELLA exits to kitchen.

THEO: – up and down over rock and stone. End of a hot day. Not a sign of him. Soon found myself at the next cove. I began to grow a little worried, needless to say. Wondered if I'd ever find him.

TOM: Couldn't give us a hotser, Walls, tea's a bit lukeish.

THEO: Yes, Father, of course, Father. As I was saying, I was beginning to fear that maybe he hadn't slipped and fallen in the water. It's hard to describe the fears that pass through your mind, when it comes to your children –

TOM: Milk.

THEO: Yes. Of course.

MAN: I used to lie awake in the dorm at night dreaming that my father'd come looking for me.

Pause.

Brought up in a home.

THEO: Tom was a great man for the homes in his day. Weren't you Tom?

JOHN enters from door that leads to hall, stairs and landing. He refills his mug. He is brought up short, however by the absence of mince pies.

JOHN: Who ate all the pies?

Silence.

Who ate all the mince pies?

Pause.

(*To THEO.*) Pig! (*To MAN.*) And you, who are you?

THEO: He's the Man –

MAN: From Oakwood. I was asking your mother if perhaps any of you had heard anything during the night.

JOHN: Apart from the celestial choirs of angels singing; 'Hosanna! Hosanna! Christ our saviour is born' ?

MAN: Yes.

JOHN: No.

MAN: You slept soundly through the night?

JOHN: Did I say that?

MAN: No, but –

JOHN: I was working –

MAN: Working?

JOHN: I'm writing a book.

MAN: I like a good read. What's it about?

JOHN: The evolution of human society from the primeval soup of the Cambrian age to its current pinnacle of achievement here in suburban Dublin. I am trying to capture that sense of loss that we all carry about within us; the loss of that innocent time when we swam through the mire as happy as divalves in shite.

MAN: My favourites are whodunits.

JOHN: Are they?

MAN: And romances.

JOHN: Bit of an old softy? What about comedies?

MAN: I like a laugh.

JOHN: And tragedies?

MAN: With happy endings.

JOHN: Of course. Got to have a happy ending. Well, I'd love to stand here all day discussing the relative merits of the various literary genres, but I'm going to go down the petrol station to get some more mince pies.

TOM: Good man yourself.

JOHN: There's a girl there, works evenings, name of Linda. Grand pair of tits on her, Tom, you'd like her. Been trying to ride her for weeks –

THEO: (*Severely.*) John, he's a Jesuit!

JOHN: Give us some money, Pig!

THEO: Yes, of course.

THEO does as ordered. He only has a few coins. JOHN takes everything he has then puts on a thin jacket and exits by hall door. Pause. MAN gets back to work. Pause.

Where was I?

TOM: While we're waiting for him, Walls, you wouldn't go see if Stella has any more of those chocolate covered Swiss rolls I had Sunday week ago?

THEO: Yes, Tom, of course.

TOM: Much appreciated Walls.

THEO gets up and exits to kitchen.

So, was it Jarleth's or Laurence's

Pause.

MAN: St. Laurence O'Toole's.

TOM: How long are you left?

Pause.

How long ago did you leave, boy?

MAN: Twenty-one years.

TOM: Come here and let me touch your face. I have become more adept at it with time.

MAN: I'd prefer not –

TOM: How am I to know whether I knew you?

MAN: You aren't. You didn't.

TOM: You can tell. There's something in the quality of the voice. Come on, let me feel you, boy. We weren't all perverts, you know –

THEO enters from kitchen.

THEO: Having a nice chat? No luck on the Cadbury's mini-rolls, Tom. That's what Stella was telling me they're called.

TOM: Quakers and Jews! Why is it Catholics never made the grade as confectioners?

THEO: Well, Johnny'll be back with some mince pies soon.

TOM: Unless he gets a ride on the filly. Make the seat of your pants stick to your backside with the sweat on a hot day, haha!

THEO: I was beginning to get a little worried. There I was, all the way to the next cove, sun beginning to go down – Did I say it was getting on for evening? Well it was getting on for evening. Then, in the distance, right at the end of the next beach, I saw a little figure with a fishing net –

MAN: Your son?

THEO: My eldest son, Joseph.

MAN: Must have been a magic moment, Mr Walls. Finding your son like that.

THEO: Yes. Yes I suppose it was.

STELLA enters from kitchen.

THEO: I thought my heart –

STELLA: Your heart? Lord preserve us! Haven't you finished yet?

THEO: (*To himself.*) I thought my heart would burst with love –

STELLA: You'll have to let me tidy up. Joseph, and his wife are due in any minute.

STELLA quickly loads the tray with tea things.

MAN: Thanks a lot for the tea, Mrs Walls.

STELLA: Not at all.

MAN: Hit the spot. And the story, Mr Walls –

THEO: But I hadn't finished –

STELLA: Save it till later, Theo. One of your memories is more than enough for anyone in one day. The Man has work to do.

MAN: Yes, Mrs Walls.

STELLA: (*To MAN.*) Well?

MAN: Well, should be done in a couple of hours. But first, I'd better have a look at your drains.

STELLA: If you must. This way, through the kitchen –

MAN: Cheers, Mrs Walls.

STELLA: I beg your pardon.

MAN: Sorry. Turn of phrase. The drains.

STELLA and the MAN exit to kitchen. Pause.

THEO: It was tough going, over the rocks, on the way back to the beach by our caravan park. And Joseph was tired, so I took him on my shoulders. As I picked my way, he must have been looking over the sea to the horizon, the setting sun –

TOM: (*By rote.*) Is that line the end of the world?

THEO: Is that line the end of the world, Daddy? No, I told him, the earth is round son, it doesn't end.

TOM: (*Ditto.*) What would happen if I swam out?

THEO: If I swam out to that line then –

TOM: You know of course this is all impossible fancy.

THEO: Excuse me, Tom?

TOM: If you were looking at the setting sun you'd be looking west. But since Wicklow faces east, it would be impossible to stand on a headland in that aforementioned county and look at the sun setting behind the sea.

Pause.

Perhaps you were out west; Donegal, or Kerry –

THEO: No, it was definitely Wicklow, 1971, had to be. I can see the rocks at my feet and the sea and the sail boat far out on the sea and the sun like a big red…like a big red tomato – And I was happy, contentment like I'd never known. You don't forget a thing like that.

TOM: The sail wasn't there before.

THEO: I'd forgotten that, until now. You see, more clues.

TOM: But clues to what, Walls, clues to what? You keep going over the same damned story?

Pause.

God help us poor bastards.

THEO: Lord graciously hear us.

TOM: Jesus!

Pause.

I knew such a moment once. Contentment. Substantiality; that kind of thing. It was in the North. Before it all started and the Father Provincial got the willies and pulled us out. The Antrim Coast. It was spring. An evening. And I'd just played the most perfect eighteen holes, taking fifty pounds off a civil servant named MacSweeney –

THEO: There's a coincidence –

TOM: Mac, Walls, Mac. He was one of them.

THEO: A queer?

TOM: A Prod. We dined on shellfish in a waterfront restaurant. And then I took a stroll down the strand, smoking a Romeo y Julietta that MacSweeney had given me. And for a few moments, that stroll on the strand, with the water aglow in the burning dusk, I had a sense, a sense of something substantial, a presence, if you like; for the briefest of moments it seemed possible that this fantastical story of salvation, that I had pissed away my life upon, it seemed possible that there was a grain of truth to it after all.

THEO: Of course there is Father, there must be.

TOM: You think? Someone out there listening to our hapless cries?

THEO: I think that's what Stella fears. People out there, in the dark, watching her.

TOM: If only it were true –

The lights go out. The lights go back on, everything is the same as before except that the wall, stage right, to the hall, stairs and upstairs is gone, leaving simply blackness.

Is it later?

THEO: No later than it would have been.

TOM: I had this awful sense that something had happened. Isn't that son of yours back yet?

THEO: Joseph?

TOM: The other one, the one with the pies.

THEO: No.

TOM: You're a divil for losing your sons, Walls.

MAN enters from kitchen followed by STELLA.

MAN: Drains seem fine, Mrs –

STELLA: We should thank heaven for –

They both stop dead.

STELLA: Theo – ?

THEO: Yes dear? (*Realising.*) O.

STELLA: How could you let this happen? How could you?

THEO: I wasn't aware –

STELLA: No, you weren't aware, were you? You were never aware, of…of…of anything. As if losing one wasn't bad enough. As if being on display to anyone who might be passing wasn't bad enough. As if being exposed for all the world to see wasn't – and I've been trying all day, trying to put a brave face on it, to carry on as normal and not give anything away. Now the world and his mother will be able to take a squint at us. And Joseph? What's he to think? O my God, his wife. And she's English. This is the living end, after all the years of…of…now this –

TOM: Lost another one, Walls? Knock another few thousand off the value.

STELLA: My God! My God!

TOM: Why hast thou forsaken me?

STELLA: Shut up!

THEO: Stella, he's a Jesuit –

STELLA: And you shut up too, you useless…useless – my God! my God! – and none of you with any comfort for me – Fine help you and your damned Oakwood have been –

MAN: There's some new equipment down the yard.

STELLA: The yard? You're not going to leave us? What's wrong with the equipment you have here? What about your tools? What about your toolbox?

STELLA goes to the toolbox. The MAN gets to it first.

MAN: It's just more complicated than I thought. I'll be back.

STELLA: Don't leave us. Please. I don't think I'll be able to keep this up –

The MAN is just about to open the door when the bell rings. Pause. STELLA pulls herself together, goes to the hall door and opens it. JOSEPH and his wife are standing there.

Joseph! And you must be Mary.

TOM: No room at the inn! No room at the inn! Haha!

TOM cackles, lights out.

End of Act One.

ACT TWO

Lights come on. The scene is as before. STELLA and MARY sit on the sofa. There are tea things on the coffee table.

MARY: – Please.

STELLA: But I'm sure I don't remember.

MARY: Once you start, it will all come back.

STELLA: Do you think?

MARY: I'm sure.

STELLA: Right, then.

MARY: Right.

STELLA: I'll give it a try then.

MARY: Do, please.

STELLA: Right. (*Pause.*) What a to-do to die today – (*Pause.*)

MARY: That's it.

STELLA: – at a minute or two to two
    A thing distinctly hard to say but harder still to do.
    There'll be a tattoo at twenty to two
    With a ta-ta-ta-ta taroo
    And a dragon will come and beat on his drum
    At a minute or two to two today –

STELLA/MARY: At a minute or two to two.

They laugh. Pause.

MARY: You did remember, after all.

STELLA: It all came back.

MARY: Once you started.

STELLA: After all these years. The elocution.

MARY: It's so important.

STELLA: To speak clearly.

MARY: The impression it makes.

STELLA: To make yourself understood.

MARY: So important –

STELLA: To make yourself understood.

MARY: To make the right impression.

STELLA: Yes.

> *Silence.*

MARY: Were you ever on the stage?

STELLA: I beg your pardon.

MARY: On the stage. Were you ever on the stage? With your accomplishments –

STELLA: No. I was never on a stage. No.

> *Silence.*

MARY: I'm sure you would have been very good.

STELLA: Do you?

MARY: I'm sure.

STELLA: I'm not so sure. I'm not sure I'd know what to say.

> *Silence.*

MARY: Well, at least they're back.

STELLA: (*Panicked.*) Who are?

MARY: The lights.

STELLA: (*Relieved.*) O them.

MARY: Joseph must have found the fuse.

STELLA: Yes. Yes, I knew we could rely on Joseph.

Pause.

I don't know what you must think of us, really I don't. I did so want everything to be nice and now you must think we all live like animals, or something.

Silence.

MARY: I'm very fond of animals.

STELLA: I'm so glad.

MARY: And my own family's from Ireland.

STELLA: You'd never know.

MARY: A long way back.

STELLA: Ascendancy?

MARY: Yes. I suppose –

STELLA: Well in that case –

MARY: I'm sure things will be fine, Stella –

STELLA: Yes. Yes. I'm sure things will be fine too, with Joseph here, now, and you, and it is a such a relief that you are just as I hoped you would be when I did have fears that you might not be as I hoped you would be. But you, here, now, just as I hoped you would be, after all. (*Pause.*) Making such a nice impression. My mother was a great woman for making the right impression, you know. Made a better person of me, I can tell you, whether I liked it or not. I've a lot to be thankful for. Where I started. Where I got to. All her hopes and dreams. All that elocution. Girls are so much more malleable, she always said. (*Shattered.*) God! Excuse me. It's so boring to talk about oneself, don't you find?

MARY: Not at all.

Silence.

STELLA: More Earl Grey?

MARY: Thank you.

STELLA: Not at all.

MARY: I like Earl Grey.

STELLA: Do you? So do I.

MARY: Yes.

STELLA: Gives you that jizz.

MARY: When you need it.

STELLA: The bergamot.

MARY: The berga-what?

STELLA: What? O, mot! I see. A joke. I'm not very good with jokes.

MARY: I'm sure you are.

STELLA: I'm sure I'm not.

Silence. They drink their tea.

What a to-do to die…

They smile at each other. Silence.

The things one remembers whether one remembers one remembers or not…

Silence.

But there they all are. All this time. Like the dragon on his drum. Bang, bang, bang. O God, where is Joseph?

JOSEPH enters from kitchen. He is rolling down his shirtsleeves.

Ah, here's Joseph.

MARY: There you are, Joseph.

JOSEPH: Here I am.

STELLA: I knew we could rely on you, Joseph.

JOSEPH: Did what I could with the fuse, but as for the –

STELLA: Please Joseph, I can bear it so long as I don't have to think about it.

JOSEPH: And the Man?

STELLA: I would not be surprised if the last has been seen of the Man.

MARY has been standing looking out over the auditorium.

MARY: What's out there, in the dark?

STELLA/JOSEPH: The park.

MARY shivers.

JOSEPH: Are you alright, Mary?

MARY: I just remembered –

STELLA: The things one remembers –

JOSEPH: Will I get your coat?

STELLA: The heating's up full.

JOSEPH: I didn't mean –

STELLA: Lord knows what it must be costing.

JOSEPH: Sorry Mum.

STELLA: You don't want to be over there, in the dark. You don't know what or who might be over there, out there. Come back here, back into the light.

MARY: (*Returning to sofa.*) Yes, yes, I'm sorry.

JOSEPH: Where's Dad?

STELLA: Leaving Tom back.

JOSEPH: The priest?

STELLA: Yes.

JOSEPH: Must be nice for him. To have a friend.

STELLA: Must it?

Pause.

JOSEPH: You know, it's great to see you after all this time.

STELLA: Yes, Joseph. And you must want a cup of Earl Grey, after your flight.

JOSEPH: Our flight?

STELLA: Yes, your flight. You must be thirsty.

JOSEPH: I've a better idea –

STELLA: Must you? I mean, do you?

JOHN enters through hall door unnoticed by the others. He has a box of mince pies.

JOSEPH: I picked up a bottle of Gordon's. What do you all say to a G and T?

JOHN: I say spiffing good idea old chap and by the way, where's the fucking wall?

STELLA: Have you no shame?

JOHN: No, but I do have a box of inferior brand mince pies.

JOSEPH: Johnny, my old kemosabe!

JOHN: Yeah Joe, how's it going?

JOSEPH: And this is Mary. Mary, Johnny.

JOHN: The English bint?

STELLA: John, language!

JOHN: Ah yes, language; an inferior brand of oral gratification compared to say, cunnilingus.

STELLA: I don't know what you're trying to imply, John, but I'm sure they flew British Midland. Don't mind him, Mary. We do our best not to mind him.

MARY: Then I shall do my best not to as well –

JOHN: Nor your walls, Mother, nor have you been minding your walls. Whither has this latest shuffled off? Whither our hall, stairs and landing? Whither my room? Not to mention whither my book, my life's work?

STELLA: Life's work? What do you know about a life's work? Whither my life?

JOSEPH: Johnny, I think it upsets Mum when you talk about it.

JOHN: It upsets me when I talk about it.

JOSEPH: Then let's not talk about it. Let's have a G and T, kemosabe.

MARY: I could do with a G and T.

JOSEPH: G and Ts all round then.

JOSEPH exits to kitchen.

STELLA: I bought some prawn wontons from M and S. Will you be wanting them with your G and Ts, or did you bring your own KP snacks too?

MARY: I'd like some prawn wontons.

STELLA: I'll warm them up then, will I?

MARY: Yes, please, do…

STELLA: Right.

STELLA leaves. MARY stands. Silence. JOHN and MARY stare out into the auditorium.

JOHN: Makes for quite a vista, during the day.

MARY: Is that so? But what about at night?

JOHN: At night it is a veritable sea of discontent.

MARY: When I was young I had nightmares.

JOHN: Is that so?

MARY: Nightmares about the sea.

JOHN: The sea of discontent?

MARY: About being out in the sea at night. Drifting further and further helpless, as the light on the shore became just a flicker, then a dot, then out.

JOHN: When I was young I had a horse.

MARY: Is that so? I like horses. I wouldn't have taken you for a horseman.

JOHN: It was more like a hobby.

MARY: Equestrianism?

JOHN: No. It was a hobby horse. Do you ride?

MARY: Horses?

JOHN: Yes, horses. Do you ride horses?

MARY: No. No I don't.

JOHN: Funny, you struck me as someone who rides. Someone experienced in that line. Someone who could handle a big horse of a thing between her legs –

MARY: Your book, tell me about –

JOHN: I loved it. Up and down, up and down, as happy as the day was dull –

MARY: Your book, your life's work? What was it about?

JOHN: O that. It was about my life.

MARY: Your life. Must be thrilling.

JOHN: It was about loss. About loss and love in the suburbs. About loss of love in the suburbs. It has realised its potential and gone and lost itself in the suburbs.

MARY: You're hard.

JOHN: I was just talking to Linda.

MARY: Your girlfriend?

JOHN: A dumb cow who works down the garage.

MARY: She resisted your charms?

JOHN: She thinks I'm a prick.

MARY: A prick?

JOHN: A big prick.

MARY: A big prick? How big a prick?

JOSEPH enters with four gin and tonics.

JOHN: The biggest one you've ever seen.

JOSEPH: You two having a nice chat?

MARY: Really? That big?

JOSEPH: What? What's that big?

JOHN: A horse. As big as a big horse of a thing. Do you remember my horse, Joseph?

JOSEPH: Your horse?

JOHN: My hobby horse. Do you remember how I'd ride up and down, up and down as happy as – do you not remember? Drove you demented. Drove him demented.

JOSEPH: No. No, I don't remember.

JOHN: You don't remember? You don't remember my hobby horse? My hobby horse which you broke in two and threw over the garden wall?

JOSEPH: You should get out more.

JOHN: I can't.

JOSEPH: See something of the world.

JOHN: But I can't.

JOSEPH: Thirty years of age, why the hell not?

JOHN: Because you broke my horse.

JOSEPH: Up in your room all day, wallowing in the past.

JOHN: It's my hobby. The only hobby I have left.

JOSEPH: Don't believe anything he says. There never was a hobby horse.

STELLA enters from kitchen carrying a tray of steaming wontons and other warm finger foods.

STELLA: That old thing. You should have seen Joseph's face when he first saw it on Christmas morning. His little face lit up. He was never off the foolish thing. Up and down. Up and down. Whatever happened to it?

JOHN: Melted to air.

JOSEPH: G and Ts everyone.

STELLA: Prawn wontons. Freshly microwaved. Where on earth is Theo?

THEO enters through hall door. Hangs up coat.

THEO: Here I am.

STELLA: There you are.

THEO: I stayed with him for a bit.

STELLA: I don't know why you don't just move in.

THEO: I think, deep down, he's afraid.

STELLA: What's he got to be afraid of? He's got God on his side. Not to mention a more than adequate pension.

THEO: But he wouldn't be able to see if something similar happened –

STELLA: Theo, please. We are not blind to our shortcomings, but we need not be reminded of them.

JOSEPH: Dad, how the hell are you?

THEO: Joseph! You know it gives your mother and myself great pleasure to see you doing so well, with your lovely wife –

JOSEPH: Mary.

THEO: (*Shaking her hand awkwardly.*) Mary.

JOSEPH: Well it gives me great pleasure…well, to come home. G and T, Dad?

THEO: G and Ts is it? With a slice of lemon and all. Isn't he the great man with his G and Ts and his lovely English wife and all those things?

JOSEPH exits to kitchen.

THEO: (*To the retreating JOSEPH.*) I was telling Tom and the Man from Oakwood earlier about the time we lost you on the beach –

STELLA: (*To MARY.*) Pay no attention dear, he never gets anywhere.

THEO: But that's the strangest thing. I remembered a new bit, on the way home. The party. There was to be a party, on the beach that night.

STELLA: Why must you do this to me?

THEO: What dear?

STELLA: I'm sure Mary is not interested, Theo.

MARY: O, I am, I'm sure. Joseph never told me about that time.

JOHN: That's because it was me.

THEO: It was the summer of '70, or '71 at the latest. You'd have been too young.

JOHN: Pig!

JOSEPH enters.

JOSEPH: Here you go, Dad.

THEO: Ah, great man. And I told you the story of Apollo, Joseph, as you sat on my shoulders, and we looked at the setting sun. I told you how he pulled the sun across the sky with his chariot. And how his son – what's this his name was?

JOSEPH: ?

JOHN: Phaeton.

THEO: That's it, Phaeton. How his son Phaeton stole his father's chariot but could not control it. And there was to be a party on the beach that night. Friends coming down from Dublin. George and poor Frances Cunningham –

STELLA: Theo! Talk of these ghosts is of no interest to our guests –

MARY: No really, I wish I knew more about my family.

STELLA: Do you really?

JOHN: Do you honestly – ?

MARY: I lost my mother when I was very young.

STELLA: There, that will teach you to be sarcastic to visitors. We seem to be surrounded by orphans this evening, dear. The Man from Oakwood was brought up in a home.

JOHN: I was brought up in a home.

STELLA: Not a real home.

JOHN: You shouldn't be so hard on yourself, Mother.

STELLA: Theo, Joseph was telling me in the kitchen he plans to go out on his own after Christmas –

JOSEPH: It's just an idea –

THEO: I had my own business once, you know –

MARY: Mary.

THEO: *Mary.* I was in big underpants.

STELLA: Underwear, Theo.

THEO: Stella Maris. Star of the Sea. Named the company after Stella. And the Virgin Mary. People are very particular about their underwear. Don't want to be run over in the wrong pair.

JOHN: Are you particular about your underwear, Mary?

JOSEPH: Johnny –

STELLA: I do not think it is appropriate that you go into your brother's wife's underwear.

MARY: It's alright, Stella, I get my underclothing from Mark's and Spencer's.

STELLA: Of course you do. Of course she does. Very sensible reply. Very sensible underwear. And what's your line to be, Joseph?

JOSEPH: Finance. Advice. I haven't quite ironed out the details. Like I said, it's only an idea –

STELLA: I'm sure it will be a very good idea, when it fully occurs to you.

Pause.

JOHN: Need a few underpants full of financial advice around here.

STELLA: Can we please leave under garments out of it. And personal finances. Money is such an uninteresting subject.

JOSEPH: But you and Dad are alright aren't you?

STELLA: Yes, yes we're fine. There's your father's small pension. And the house, what's left of it –

THEO: Tom thinks the situation might affect the value –

STELLA: And of course the money you invested for us, in Summersfield.

MARY: Summersfield – ?

THEO: His father's eye for an opening.

JOHN: Isn't he the great man?

THEO: Great man indeed.

STELLA: Anyway, we can talk about it later.

JOSEPH: Yes. Later.

STELLA: At an appropriate time.

JOSEPH: When we get a chance –

MARY: But Summersfield –

JOSEPH: Later, Mary. It's great to see you after all this time, Mum, Dad –

STELLA: Yes, Joseph you said that.

Silence. Lights go, momentarily, then return.

THEO: Is it later?

STELLA: No later than it would have been.

JOSEPH: I'm sorry, I was sure I'd fixed that –

STELLA: Well, if nothing else has given way or fallen apart, someone please say something.

JOHN: –

STELLA: Something nice. Perhaps you would like to tell us how you met, Mary?

JOHN: I was simply going to remark that my glass is empty.

JOSEPH: So it is. Perhaps you would care to refill it.

JOHN: Perhaps the great man with his ice and lemon would.

JOSEPH: Perhaps you'd care to take a flying –

MARY: Joseph, perhaps, since it is our gin –

JOSEPH: Well, perhaps since he likes to drink our gin.

MARY: Well perhaps I'd like another gin too, Joseph.

Pause.

JOSEPH: Perhaps I should get another round, then.

JOSEPH gets up collects everyone's glasses and exits to kitchen.

STELLA: Now Mary, you were going to tell us how you two met.

JOHN: Yes Mary, please pray tell us, how you two met?

MARY: At a meet.

JOHN: You met at a meet? Mother, they met at a meet.

STELLA: A meet?

MARY: A horse meet.

JOHN: Horse meat? I thought only the French –

MARY: An equestrian event.

JOHN: And were you riding at this event?

MARY: I was not riding, I was spectating.

JOHN: Did I tell you I used to ride?

MARY: You told me.

STELLA: And that's where you met Joseph?

MARY: Yes –

JOHN: I take it he was not riding. Joseph was never one for riding. Quite anti-riding, if I remember correctly –

MARY: He was spectating –

JOHN: At the riding event?

MARY: The meet.

STELLA: John, I'm having great difficulty following the story.

JOHN: I apologise, Mother. I apologise, Mary. Continue please, I pray you.

MARY: We were at the rail by the finishing line. We found we were cheering the same horse. It was very exciting. He led from the off. The horse. Down to the finishing straight. He'd only the last to jump. But then, he fell. Broke his leg. They had to destroy him. Summersfield. The horse's name. Summersfield. Such a tragedy –

THEO: There's a coincidence. The name of the company Joseph invested our money in –

MARY: So it's not the same?

STELLA: The same? I should hope not. No. Summersfield's a new development Joseph got a hot tip on.

THEO: His father's eye for an opening.

MARY: That is a relief, you see I thought –

JOSEPH enters with drinks.

STELLA: Mary was telling us how you met.

JOHN: At the meet.

STELLA: And the horse.

JOHN: Summersfield –

JOSEPH: We'll talk later, I said –

JOHN: How it died. The horse –

MARY: And when your mother had mentioned before about your investing their money in Summersfield too and I thought she'd meant the horse –

STELLA: A horse! A horse! Our savings on a horse!

JOHN: Destroyed. Like my hobby horse.

STELLA: Well, at least we've cleared that up, and apart from the horse –

JOHN: The dead horse –

STELLA: I'm sure it was most romantic.

MARY: It was. Yes. I suppose. And in fact then we did really discover the most amazing coincidence.

THEO: Another coincidence. Isn't he a great man for the coincidences? Aren't you a great man for the coincidences, Joseph?

JOSEPH: Mary's father was Frank.

THEO: I've always tried to be frank as a father.

JOSEPH: No, Frank, my boss.

THEO: That is another coincidence. And smart move, son, marrying the boss's daughter.

JOSEPH: I married Mary because I loved her.

STELLA: Of course you did. Of course he loved her, Theo.

JOSEPH: I do love her.

STELLA: He still does love her, Theo.

THEO: Of course, of course he did, of course you do. But smart move all the same. Had things been different, myself and Frances Cunningham, poor George Cunningham's wife –

STELLA: Can't we leave your sordid past out of it, Theo? We were doing quite nicely there for a bit. Please, someone have something. They'll soon be stone cold. There's vol-au-vents too. You must be ravenous after your flight, will you have a vol-au-vent?

MARY: But we didn't fly.

STELLA: Of course you did.

THEO: Of course. Of course he did. Of course you do –

STELLA: Theo!

JOSEPH: Well, we didn't. I was going to tell you later.

STELLA: But how did you get here?

JOSEPH: The boat.

STELLA: The ferry?

JOSEPH: The car ferry.

STELLA: You mustn't have booked in time. I believe it's murder trying to get a flight this time of year with all the ghosts crawling out of the woodwork. I mean the returning emigrants. Excuse me, I don't know what I was thinking –

MARY: It doesn't really matter how we got here, anyway.

STELLA: So long as you're here.

MARY: That's what's important.

STELLA: That's what counts.

JOSEPH: And Dad, we haven't had a chance to talk. It's great to see you.

THEO: And you too, with your pretty wife, and your successful career, and all those things.

JOSEPH: I'm sure Johnny's doing well, in his own way.

JOHN: Well I'm sure he's not.

STELLA: Well your brother's only trying to be nice.

JOHN: Well I'm not trying to be anything.

STELLA: Well at the very least, you could try to remember where you are.

JOHN: In the relative privacy of what was once my own home.

STELLA: The situation. Remember the situation.

JOHN: There has always been some situation. I cannot remember a time when there has not been a situation –

STELLA: We have never had a situation like this situation, let me assure you, Mary. Some people take great pleasure in seeing other people in situations like this, I can tell you, in watching other people suffer. God knows who could be out there, waiting, watching for one of us to slip up, hoping for some new disaster to befall us so they can go home smug in the knowledge, smug in the knowledge of having seen other people suffer, seen other people in some situation or other. I'm sorry.

MARY: I know just the kind of people you mean, Stella.

STELLA: I'm glad someone, at least, knows what I mean.

JOHN: Well why don't we give the poor bastards something to see then?

JOHN starts howling like a dog.

STELLA: What on earth do you think you are doing?

JOHN: Crying for help into the sea of discontent.

JOHN recommences.

JOSEPH: Johnny, come on –

STELLA: You are being ridiculous.

JOHN: Let he who is without ridiculousness cast the first stone.

JOHN recommences.

STELLA: Stop it! Stop it! Or leave my house.

JOHN: Before it leaves me. Yes, yes of course. I'm sorry. I was forgetting the conventions of our situation, Mother. I apologise Mother for interrupting your performance.

STELLA: I really do hope there's no one out there. I don't know what you must think, Mary, that we live in a zoo, or something.

MARY: I don't agree with zoos.

STELLA: I know. Cruel, inhuman places. We should be free.

MARY: Don't you mean 'they'?

STELLA: Yes, they. They should be free.

MARY: But you said 'we'.

STELLA: We? Why would I say 'we'? We're not animals. We are free.

JOHN: But find ourselves everywhere in chains –

STELLA: Shut up. Theo, Theo you've been very quiet. Say something.

THEO: I was thinking. About the party. And Frances Cunningham.

STELLA: That old tart. Excuse the language but I can't go on like this. It's as though a huge iron fist were squeezing my heart. Sometimes I feel as though I cannot breathe. And if I were to shout for help, no sound would emerge. So you didn't book in time?

JOSEPH: We did. In October. When I told you we were coming.

STELLA: The airplane, I meant.

JOSEPH: The car ferry.

STELLA: You know we will not think the less of you for taking the ferry.

MARY: We thought we'd take the car. That's why we booked the car ferry. See something of the country. My family's from Ireland –

STELLA: Yes, you said. I'm sorry. I knew there would be some perfectly reasonable explanation why you took the ferry.

JOHN: Just so long as you're here, that what's important.

STELLA: That's what matters.

THEO: So what are you driving these days, Joseph?

JOSEPH: We did have…an Audi.

THEO: An Audi. There's a coincidence. That's what I drove in my prime. In my heyday. German engineering –

MARY: *Vursprung durch tecknik*, as they say in Germany.

THEO: *Ich komme mit unterhosen in allen grossen*, as I used to say in Germany. We sold to the Germans. Underpants, not cars. Though you'd be hard pushed to beat a Japanese these days, Tom says. Never sold underpants to the Japanese. I expect they take smaller sizes.

STELLA: Theo, for the love of God –

THEO: Though I didn't see your car outside when I was coming back from Tom's –

JOSEPH: We were going to bring it. That was the plan. But we got rid of it.

THEO: My first Audi was chocolate coloured. An unfortunate choice in the underpants game. I got rid of it, for a red one. Is that why you got rid of yours?

JOSEPH: No. We're between cars at present.

MARY: It was like a company car. And since Joseph is going out on his own –

JOSEPH: It's only an idea –

JOHN howls.

STELLA: Don't mind him, Mary, he always wants to be the centre of attention.

MARY: In fact we were thinking of moving to Dublin. Things are on the up, we hear.

STELLA: What? Why on earth would you want to do that? You were doing so well over there –

JOSEPH: Mary, we can talk about it later. Johnny, will you stop? You are upsetting your mother.

JOHN: (*Stops.*) Don't know about you, but I feel a bit better now I got that off my chest.

THEO: The Walls, back in business in Dublin, it makes your mother and myself proud –

A dog howls from the auditorium.

And all those things –

STELLA: What was that?

THEO: What was what, dear?

STELLA: This is too much, this is simply too much –

JOSEPH: It's probably just some poor lost stray in the park.

STELLA: This time you've gone too far. There's something out there, I know there is.

JOSEPH: There's nothing out there, Mum, there's nothing out there. Let's all sit down and have another drink.

JOSEPH collects all the glasses.

JOHN: What I don't understand is why you didn't fly when it became apparent that you would no longer have the use of your company car?

JOSEPH: (*Leaving to kitchen.*) Because we'd already bought the tickets.

JOHN: So that's the answer, Mr Great Man Yourself; thrift. Did you learn that in economics? Or was it Economy of Truth, you were taking that term? But do they let you on a car ferry with a car ticket if you have no car?

STELLA: What must you think, Mary?

JOHN: Yes, Mary, what must you think?

MARY: I don't know what to think.

JOHN: And I'm damned if I know what to think of it.

JOSEPH enters with gin and tonics.

JOSEPH: There's no ice and no lemons.

JOHN: Enlighten us Joe, we don't know what to think.

JOSEPH: You never did. Happy Christmas, Dad.

THEO: There was to be a party that night. On the beach.

JOSEPH: Mary, are you okay?

MARY: Yes. No. Stop asking me that.

JOSEPH: Here little brother, take this drink and shut up.

MARY: What party? What night, Mr Walls?

THEO: The night of the day that I lost Joseph and found him.

JOHN: It was me, Pig, it was me. Though I sometimes wish you'd never found me.

THEO: Everyone was there; the neighbours from the caravan park, friends coming down from Dublin, and a huge bonfire on the beach –

STELLA: As though a huge iron fist were squeezing my heart –

THEO: By the time we'd scrambled down the rocks, back to the beach, the moon was out. Blood red. Like a huge… tomato. And the great bonfire was lit.

STELLA: Why? Why do you have to come back? We gave you everything you needed to succeed. Somewhere else.

THEO: And as we approached the fire we could see figures, shadows, there were guitars, we heard singing;

(*Sings the first few lines of The Carpenters' 'Top of the World'.*) *Such a change is coming over me…etc.*

STELLA: Make him stop, Joseph, please make him stop.

JOSEPH: Dad?

THEO: That song. It was big at the time. The things you remember. It's all coming back.

THEO continues to sing.

STELLA: (*Over THEO's singing.*) And I so wanted everything to be nice.

JOSEPH: It is nice, Mum, it is. We just need a little to get us started, that's all.

STELLA: But we don't have anything more to give you.

THEO: (*Breaking off singing.*) And there, come down specially all the way from Dublin for the night, was the bould Sweeney –

Lights out. THEO continues to sing. Lights on. The back wall with the hall door is gone. A figure stands in the relative obscurity.

What is the next line?

JOSEPH: Another one.

STELLA: Where will it all end?

MARY: There's someone there.

STELLA: Who is? Who's there?

JOSEPH: O my God, Mr Sweeney!

MARY: Daddy!

THEO: Sweeney!

STELLA: Frank?

THEO: Frank Sweeney –

STELLA: After all these years.

Slowly SWEENEY comes downstage. Pause. He collapses. Blackout.

End of Act Two.

ACT THREE

The lights return. SWEENEY lies motionless on the coffee table. THEO and STELLA sit as in the previous act. JOHN stands as before. JOSEPH paces up and down. MARY stands downstage staring out at auditorium. The armchair is missing.

STELLA: O God, they're back.

THEO: It was longer this time. Fifteen, twenty minutes.

STELLA: Where's it all going to end?

THEO: Worse before it gets better.

STELLA: Worse? How much worse – ?

JOSEPH: What about the kitchen?

THEO: Still there, for the moment –

JOSEPH: I mean him. Put him in the kitchen.

STELLA: That would be unhygienic.

JOHN: At least here he is only unaesthetic.

MARY: What the hell is he doing here in the first place.

JOHN: Very little, it would seem.

STELLA: We must try to carry on as normal.

THEO: I must say, it is a coincidence. Him showing up here after all this time. And me only talking about him. Your mother didn't think of making the trip too, did she dear?

STELLA: Theo, Mary has already told us that she lost her mother.

THEO: Like I lost Joseph.

JOSEPH: Shouldn't we call someone?

STELLA: The phone was in the hall, Joseph.

JOSEPH: We should do something about him, Mary.

MARY: Chuck him over the garden wall with your brother's horse, for all I care.

JOSEPH: What horse?

STELLA: Your stock isn't quite as Ascendant as I had imagined, dear.

MARY: We do our best to better ourselves.

JOSEPH: Well I'm not staying here with him –

MARY: That's great, that is. Here I am, trying all evening to put a brave face on it, trying not to give anything away, trying to carry on as if all this, this was normal, and first sign of trouble and you're out of here. You were the one meant to get me out of –

JOSEPH: I was going to the kitchen to get more G and Ts.

MARY: G ant Ts! Bloody barman, that's all you're good for –

STELLA: He has a degree, I should hope he's good for a lot more –

JOSEPH: Who's for a refill?

JOHN: Don't mind if I do, brother.

JOSEPH: Didn't think you would.

JOHN: Well I don't.

JOSEPH: Don't you?

JOHN: No.

THEO: And there's another coincidence, Sweeney being your boss, not to mention your wife…

ALL: Mary.

THEO: – your wife *Mary*'s father.

JOSEPH collects glasses and leaves.

JOHN: Not to mention the coincidence of our family name and our fatal structural flaw, *O pater noster.*

STELLA: I do not think we need reminding –

JOHN: Then again, perhaps it's not such a coincidence.

STELLA: Of course it is. Now, can we change the subject – ?

JOHN: Well is it not all a bit too coincidental, these coincidences happening at the same time?

STELLA: No, it is simply a coincidence of coincidences coinciding coincidentally in my bloody front room. I'm sorry. Maybe I shouldn't have another. What else could it be?

JOHN: All I mean is that perhaps there is some reason, some meaning to all these coincidences.

STELLA: Like someone intended it.

JOHN: Even if only subconsciously intended –

STELLA: I know what you're trying to imply, you're trying to imply that we somehow intended it, that I intended it, that I intended it and am therefore to blame for this. I know you. I know your style. That's what you're trying to imply. Well you can just stop trying to imply that right now because, let me tell you this, because this is the last, the very last thing that I would want or wish to happen – him, it, us, any of it, I'd sooner be, be buried alive than, than any of this. I'll tell you, I'll tell you this for nothing, if someone was to blame for this it would not surprise me who that someone might be, up in his room all day, plotting –

JOHN: Plotting my novel, Mother, plotting my novel –

STELLA: It's not natural. Thirty years of age. You should get out in the world. You had all the chances your brother had –

JOHN: And what's he got to show for it –

STELLA: A job, a wife –

THEO: *Mary.*

STELLA: Thank you, Theo but I know her bloody name. I beg your pardon, Mary. You should make something of yourself.

JOHN: I have, Mother, a mess.

STELLA: What did I ever do to you that you treat me like this?

JOHN: You bore me.

STELLA: Well, if it's any consolation, you bore me too.

JOSEPH enters with drinks.

JOHN: The great man himself!

JOSEPH: The bottle's nearly –

MARY: Ssshhh. I hear something. Doesn't anyone else hear something?

A distant humming is heard. It might possibly be a song.

A distant humming.

STELLA: Theo? Is that you?

THEO: Is what me dear?

STELLA: The noise. The distant humming. You're not intending to sing again, I hope.

THEO: No dear, I can't seem to remember the second verse –

STELLA: Thanks heavens for small mercies.

MARY: It's him.

STELLA: Must he do that?

SWEENEY is humming. Gradually the humming becomes a song, 'Top of the World.'

SWEENEY: (*Concluding.*) *Your love's put me at the top of the...*

Pause.

JOSEPH: Mr Sweeney?

STELLA: Frank –

SWEENEY: What? Where? Stella? (*Sitting up.*) The dead arose and appeared to many, what? Lord, I've been travelling. A million miles. Off with the birds.

STELLA: Well, you are back on *terra firma* now, and while we rejoice in your recovery, Frank, the singing –

SWEENEY: No worries on that score, Stella, can't for the life of me think what comes next.

THEO: Me neither, Sweeney, me neither. Isn't that a coincidence?

SWEENEY: Hundred thousand apologies for the entrance Stella, Theo. Compliments of the season to you all. And my little Trixie –

MARY: Don't call me that.

SWEENEY: Don't be like that with your old Dad, and me after one of my turns.

STELLA: After our initial surprise we saw that you were breathing comfortably and weren't swallowing your tongue or anything foolish like that. We were sure you'd pull through.

SWEENEY: And a hundred thousand thanks for the ministrations, Stella. They've been coming more regular of late. The turns. The quack says it's the old ticker. Should take it easy –

MARY: Well then, what are you doing running about after me for?

SWEENEY: I'll ignore that.

STELLA: We find ignorance is the best policy. That didn't quite sound how I meant it to sound –

SWEENEY: After all I've done for her, after all I've suffered, the ingratitude of children, Stella –

STELLA: We ourselves possess the object lesson –

JOHN: I object.

SWEENEY: I gave you everything you ever needed. I've worked and I've suffered. (*To JOSEPH.*) And you, you ungrateful little… After all I've done for you, too. Give us a drink here, my throat's as dry as a nun's…hundred thousand apologies, Stella.

STELLA: One will suffice.

SWEENEY: What is this? Is it a girl's perfume you'd have me drink? You know I've lived amongst the enemy for twenty-five year, but I've never acquired their infernal tastes. There's a bottle of Irish in the bag there. Fetch it over. (*He looks around.*) This is a quare old place youse are living in. What's this that's out there?

ALL: The park.

SWEENEY: Must make for a quite a vista. During the day. And, if you don't mind me asking, in the absence of three of your walls, what would be holding your roof up?

JOHN: Faith, hope and –

STELLA: Spite.

THEO: I was just saying there Sweeney, while you were off with your birds, that it's quite a coincidence you showing up here after all these years and me only telling Tom – he's a Jesuit, lives on the Close – me only telling him about you earlier. And you being Joseph's boss, not to mention *Mary,* his wife's, father –

SWEENEY: Small world, Walls, small old world as the crow flies when it boils down to it.

MARY: And why is it you never said you might know Joey's parents? There can't be that many Joseph Bloody Walls's from Dublin –

STELLA: Mary, dear, since the somewhat melancholy arrival of your father, your linguistic standards appear to be declining alarmingly –

MARY: This is the standard I've been trying to pull myself up from all my life but he, he keeps dragging me back down.

SWEENEY: I've a good mind to take you across my knee –

STELLA: Please Frank, given the situation, I would appreciate if you would refrain from actions that might be considered ambiguous –

SWEENEY: Of course, Stella. Apologies, Stella. And you, Missy, apologise to Stella –

MARY: A hundred thousand million apologies, Stella –

SWEENEY: You know I've a good mind –

MARY: Well why didn't you tell me?

SWEENEY: I didn't like to. He was like a son to me. A bird in the hand and a sleeping dog and all that.

A dog howls from the auditorium.

What was that?

JOHN: The sleeping dog arising from his bush –

STELLA: Just some poor lost stray.

SWEENEY: Aren't we all lost strays, Stella, when it boils down to it? Looking for some place or other to alight upon and call home. Give us another lash there, you –

JOSEPH pours SWEENEY some whiskey.

JOHN: Did you take the boat, Mr Sweeney? Joseph and Mary took the boat. Didn't you Joseph?

SWEENEY: Haven't been on that tub since I upped and took wing back in '74 –

JOHN: He was going to take his car, Mr Sweeney, an Audi –

SWEENEY: Is that so? And whose Audi would that be?

STELLA: It was a company car.

SWEENEY: A company car! I suppose he did do the cash and carry run for me the odd –

THEO: I used to drive an Audi. Do you remember my Audi, Sweeney?

SWEENEY: How could I forget? Old skidmark Walls.

THEO: The red one, not the brown one. I got rid of the brown one.

SWEENEY: I remember the brown one.

THEO: He was going to drive around. Show Mary something of the place. You could have done that. Brought your wife…if she wasn't –

STELLA: Theo, you are like a bull in the china shop of peoples' emotions.

SWEENEY: It's alright, Stella. I've learned to live with my losses. No, Walls, I didn't think of travelling around. Can't afford the time off, even if I wanted.

STELLA: Of course, Frank. And how is business?

SWEENEY: Business? Business is, well, busy this time of year.

STELLA: Is it? Is it really?

SWEENEY: Everyone out on the town.

STELLA: Looking for property?

SWEENEY: Looking for a party, more like.

STELLA: In your properties?

SWEENEY: On my property –

JOSEPH: Mum, whiskey? This is our party after all –

STELLA: No Joseph, I do not want a whiskey.

THEO: A party indeed. Do you remember the party on the beach in Wicklow. '70 or '71. You were the life and the soul –

SWEENEY: No. I don't recall an occasion in Wicklow. I remember Cork or Kerry, or somewhere in that region, '74.

THEO: No, it wasn't Kerry. It was Wicklow. We never had a caravan out west. You came down from Dublin. To Wicklow.

SWEENEY: No, then, I don't remember –

THEO: And Frances Cunningham was there pouring everyone Cinzano – we had all the drinks; Cinzano, Dubonnet, Kiskadee –

STELLA: He doesn't remember, Theo.

THEO: Of course he remembers –

SWEENEY: I don't, really –

STELLA: He doesn't Theo.

JOHN: And Joseph was telling us he's planning to go out on his own, here in Dublin –

THEO: Like I was out on my own all those years ago –

JOHN: Not waving but drowning.

JOSEPH: It's only an idea –

THEO: I expect he told you. Financial advice.

SWEENEY: (*Guffawing, spraying drink.*) Financial advice! From him! Did he never tell you about the Summersfield mullarkey?

STELLA: On second thoughts, Joseph, perhaps I shall have another.

JOSEPH: Yes, Mum, of course Mum.

SWEENEY: Well, didn't you, boy – ?

JOSEPH: Yes, Mr Sweeney, I told them about Summersfield.

STELLA: Yes, thank you Frank, he did tell us about Summersfield –

JOSEPH: Earlier.

STELLA: He told us about Summersfield earlier. Now can we – ?

SWEENEY: Well then, talk about – !

STELLA: Like we said, we did talk about it –

SWEENEY: Well if you talked about it –

STELLA: Actually, it was Mary who talked about, mainly –

JOSEPH: I talked about it a little.

STELLA: And Joseph, a little. Now if you don't mind –

SWEENEY: Well then, you'll know. Talk about – !

STELLA: We talked about it. Have we not made it clear?

SWEENEY: You have, you have. So talk about – !

STELLA: Frank, you don't seem to understand. We talked about it earlier. We talked it through earlier. We talked all the talk there was to talk about it earlier and if there is anything else to say on the matter we can talk about it later. In the meantime can we talk about something else?

Pause.

SWEENEY: Of course Stella, of course (*Chuckling to himself.*) Talk about – !

THEO: A coincidence, Sweeney, talk about a coincidence. Summersfield. The horse. The property development. Talk about coincidence.

SWEENEY: What on earth are you talking about, Walls?

THEO: Coincidences. Isn't the place coming down with them tonight. I'm surprised the weatherman didn't forecast them on the weather forecast. Coincidences will be general over Ireland, falling fast and furious on the Greater Dublin region.

THEO laughs. Pause.

I'm surprised the weatherman didn't say that. Really.

STELLA: Thank you, Theo.

THEO: Don't mention it, dear.

STELLA: Now, could I not interest anyone in one of these delicious pre-prepared snacks from Marks and Spencers.

JOHN: Or one of my mince pies, from the garage. I could warm them up.

STELLA: My wontons have been warmed –

JOHN: Anyone care for a nice warm pie – ?

STELLA: – as were my vol-au-vents and mini pizzas –

JOHN: And cream, I could whip some cream –

STELLA: Would no-one care for even a vol-au-vent – ?

JOHN: Warm pies and cream –

STELLA: Someone? Anyone?

JOHN: I'll go warm the pies and whip some cream then, will I – ?

STELLA: Well if you are going, go. There's no need to make such a song and dance –

JOHN: Right, I'll go then –

JOHN exits to kitchen.

JOSEPH: I'll take a vol-au-vent, then, Mum.

STELLA: You don't have to do me any favours, Joseph.

SWEENEY: (*His interior monologue becoming audible.*) – and what thanks do I get? Runs off with my only daughter, my own and only flesh and blood, leaving me on my lonesome, at Christmas. What way is that to repay – ?

THEO: You did a grand job bringing her up, all the same.

SWEENEY: It was hard, I can tell you, after all I'd been through. The stink over that factory of yours.

THEO: Pushed it through, in spite of the residents.

SWEENEY: What became of it?

THEO: Way of all matter. Slump in underpants. Worse before it got better. Got better too late for us.

SWEENEY: Lost my job in the Corpo over that factory, my
home –

THEO: Not to mention your wife –

SWEENEY: Yes, Walls, my wife – I suffered, deep down
I suffered. But I did my best, all the same. And now what
thanks do I get? Not even a kiss, not even a cuddle.

Awkward pause.

THEO: Listen Sweeney, old man, I'm sorry about your job,
and your home, and your wife, and all those things, and
even the factory, at the end of the day, really I am, but
I can't see that a, a kiss or, or a cuddle would, well would
make things any better –

SWEENEY: Mary, Walls, a kiss and cuddle from my
daughter, Mary.

THEO: Of course. Of course you meant Mary. Simple
enough misunderstanding.

SWEENEY: Come on, my little Trixie, make an old man
happy and give him a little kiss and a cuddle –

MARY: Don't touch me –

THEO: Can't have been easy –

MARY: Don't come near me –

SWEENEY: Can say that again. But her happiness –

MARY: You disgust me.

SWEENEY: Was all that mattered to me.

MARY turns towards the kitchen.

JOSEPH: Where are you going?

MARY: The kitchen.

JOSEPH: The kitchen?

MARY: Help you brother with his pies and his cream. I've been thinking, I'd quite fancy one of his pies. With cream.

JOSEPH: Mary – ?

MARY: You know, you too are beginning to disgust me, you know that.

JOSEPH: What do you mean, Mary – ?

MARY: Talk about big pricks!

MARY exits to kitchen. Silence.

STELLA: First impressions can be so misleading, I find.

THEO: Grand job all the same, Sweeney. Lovely girl, lovely girl.

SWEENEY: (*Maudlin.*) Lovely girl! Lovely girls! All of them. All the girls.

THEO: Don't you remember Frances Cunningham at all Sweeney? She was a lovely girl? A woman even.

STELLA: Can we not lay that corpse in the long grass yet – ?

THEO: – and that night, the party on the beach, she was singing that song.

STELLA: I'm warning you, Theo –

THEO: Not that song. Another song. The Cinzano song. How's this it went?

STELLA: Any song, I'm warning you.

THEO: But I'm only making conversation, dear. Only catching up with an old friend.

STELLA: O Theo, go and check on Tom.

THEO: What?

STELLA: Look in on him. See if he's alright.

THEO: But he's a priest. I wouldn't want to interrupt him. He might be…you know…praying.

STELLA: Use his phone while you're at it. Call someone to have a look at Frank. Frank should have someone look at him –

THEO: But Sweeney's alright. You're alright Sweeney, aren't you?

SWEENEY: Still a bit up in the air, if truth be told, Walls.

STELLA: There you are. Take Tom some vol-au-vents. He'd like that.

THEO: He would like a vol-au-vent. He likes vol-au-vents.

STELLA: Go, Theo, you know you'd never forgive yourself if something happened.

THEO: Maybe I should look in on him then.

STELLA: Yes, Theo.

Sound of MARY's giggling and laughter from kitchen.

JOSEPH: Perhaps I should look in on Mary. See if she's alright.

SWEENEY: Sounds like your brother's on top of that situation.

STELLA: If it's not one situation, it's another.

JOSEPH: I'd like to see what the situation is, exactly.

STELLA: O get out of here, Joseph.

JOSEPH: Yes, Mum. Mum, I'm sorry. Next time –

STELLA: Go.

JOSEPH exits to kitchen. The laughter in the kitchen stops. THEO is standing lost where the hall door used to be.

STELLA: What is it now, Theo?

THEO: (*Quietly.*) My coat.

SWEENEY: Take mine.

STELLA: Thank you Frank.

THEO: Thank you, Sweeney. Well then…

> *THEO exits meticulously through where the hall door once was. STELLA and SWEENEY are alone. Silence. Lights flicker off then on. Silence from the kitchen. The dog howls.*

STELLA: Still lost. In the dark. Looking for home.

SWEENEY: Twenty-five years. Off with the birds.

STELLA: It seems but a moment ago. And yet again it seems as though each minute were a grain of sand passing one by one in slow procession across the desert of my life until they had measured out eternity.

> *Silence. Lights flicker off then on. Same as before but there is an argument going on in the kitchen, now. Nothing distinct, but JOSEPH is heard to raise his voice from time to time, MARY to laugh mockingly and raise her voice and mumbling pauses where JOHN is being quietly sardonic. Pause.*

I'm sorry, Frank. Your house, is it nice, your house?

SWEENEY: It does.

STELLA: Three bedroomed?

SWEENEY: Two.

STELLA: Two. I suppose you don't need any more.

SWEENEY: No.

STELLA: With Mary gone.

SWEENEY: (*Quietly.*) Yes.

STELLA: Even what you have will seem like too much.

SWEENEY: Yes.

STELLA: And thank you, for Joseph. For taking him under your wing. He doesn't deserve it. While they're away it's easier. You can imagine, at least, for the better.

SWEENEY: He was like a son to me.

STELLA: Yes, you said that.

SWEENEY: Least I could do.

STELLA: And Mary –

SWEENEY: Strangest thing, I always felt Mary had something of you about her. Your air, your –

STELLA: Strangest thing, I feel as though everything's coming apart, as though the earth is cracking open in some dance of death and everything I used to know or thought I knew is melting right away. What area did you say your house was in?

SWEENEY: Crouch End.

STELLA: Crouch End. I'm sure it's very nice.

SWEENEY: It does. I loved you.

STELLA: One of those improving areas.

SWEENEY: I think I probably still do love you.

STELLA: In the way areas improve. For the better. We had such hope. For this area. For everything. You start out with all that hope. End up so disappointed. So god-awfully disappointed.

SWEENEY: Down through the awful whirl of years, down all those years clutching at straws. You. You –

(*Sings softly from 'Top of the World'.*)
Such a feeling's coming over me…etc.

STELLA: Such an awful disappointment. All these years
believing people, places, things to have been one way,
and when one sees, when one finally sees them, the
people, the places, the things, they are otherwise, altered,
coarsened. There again, perhaps it's oneself who is
otherwise. I'm sorry. I have exceeded my usual limits.
It must be nice to have a daughter. I would have liked
a daughter. Girls are more malleable, my mother used
to say.

Pause.

A thing distinctly hard to do but harder still to say.
Please Frank, for the love of God, have a prawn wonton.
They've hardly been touched.

SWEENEY: Dance with me, Stella.

*He raises her up. Stiffly and distractedly STELLA dances
with him. He hums 'Top of the World'.*

SWEENEY: I'm an embarrassment to her. I love her and
she hates me. I never had a wife, you know. I've never
told her. She's from a home, Stella. That's why, that's
why I always thought –

STELLA: (*Harshly breaking off.*) Well don't think. Don't ever
think. What's lost is lost. What's lost cannot be found! –

*SWEENEY staggers slightly. Sits down. He is winded. JOHN
enters riding an imaginary hobby-horse. He is followed by
JOSEPH and more slowly by MARY.*

JOHN: The lone ranger rides again!

JOSEPH: What do you think you're doing?

JOHN: I'm riding my hobby-horse, what does it look like
I'm doing, kemosabe?

JOSEPH: What do you think you were doing, in there, with my wife brother?

JOHN: (*Continuing to ride.*) We were talking. Talking about riding. Fancy a ride, Mary? Up and down, up and down –

JOSEPH: You better get off that horse, brother –

THEO enters slowly, unnoticed, pushing TOM in his wheelchair. TOM is in his nightshirt, dishevelled, distractedly he eats a vol-au-vent.

THEO: He was in a state, Stella, crying. He's calmed down now. The vol-au-vent helped, but I thought it best to bring him over –

JOHN: Up and down, over rock and rock pool we stumbled and scrabbled. Him dragging me by the arm. Me, crying. Such a smacking he'd given me. The Pig! My first attempt to leave home. My last –

JOSEPH: It was me. He told me the story of Apollo. I remember –

JOHN: And it was dark by the time we made it back to the beach. There was a bonfire. And singing –

JOSEPH: You were too young –

JOHN: And they were all there. People from the caravan park. Mr Sweeney –

THEO: The life and soul –

JOHN: And George and Frances Cunningham –

TOM: Walls, are you there, Walls?

THEO: Any time, any place, any where she sang as she danced, and poured us all drinks. Cinzano, Dubonnet and Kiskadee –

TOM: Walls, I've seen it.

JOHN: They were all there. (*Quoting sarcastically.*) 'The young in one anothers' arms' –

JOHN stops, still holding his imaginary hobby horse in his hands.

THEO: It's the right one, the bright one, she sang as she danced. And she smiled, what a smile –

STELLA: And none of us saw her wander away –

THEO: Dubonnez vous, Theo, my love? She said –

STELLA: Too busy with our own petty desires and despairs –

TOM: I've seen the future and –

THEO: And she took me by the hand –

STELLA: And none of us saw her wander away –

TOM: And it's a horror show –

THEO: And I said; Stella –

SWEENEY: And I still do –

THEO: Did I say Cinzano? Because it wasn't Cinzano. It was Martini. It was the Martini song. And it wasn't Frances? Because Frances had passed away that spring. The spring of '74. Cancer. And this was the summer of '74. And it was Stella, Stella who I danced with, on that last day, of that last summer, as the whole world was set to go down the tubes. And we were out west. I remember –

STELLA: My girl, my little girl –

THEO: And Stella said; dubonnez vous, my love, my only love –

STELLA: Into the dark sea –

JOSEPH: Look what you've started, brother. Give me that horse. Give me that damned horse.

THEO: And I said, Stella, je dubonne, oui, Stella –

STELLA: Into the dark sea she wandered and we never saw her.

JOSEPH: (*Grabbing the imaginary horse.*) Look! I've got it!

THEO: Contentment like I'd never known.

JOSEPH: I've got your horse.

THEO: You don't forget a thing like that –

JOSEPH: Look, I'm going to break it. (*Breaking imaginary horse.*) Look, I've broken it. I've broken your goddamned hobby horse once and for all and I'm going to throw it away. Into the park.

STELLA: My child, my girl, my daughter –

MARY: Drifting further and further away, helpless, as the light on the shore became just a flicker, then a dot, then out –

JOSEPH: Look, I've thrown away your horse –

JOHN: What horse, kemosabe, what horse? You're imagining things.

End of Act Three.

ACT FOUR

In the darkness.

STELLA: What a to-do to die to day, at a minute or two to two.
A thing distinctly hard to say, but harder still to do.

*Lights come on. The stage is completely bare. No walls remain.
A bleak light snaps on. STELLA stands alone on the stage.
STELLA looks around.*

Well, that's the last of them. God it's cold in here. Must
be later. Very late. I think we all overdid it tonight.
Exceeded our limits. Said things we didn't mean. Did
things we didn't mean. What a to do – God it's deathly
in here. Wherever it is I am now. Yet it seems so familiar.
As though I've been here before. Night after night. Up
here. All alone. If only the Man from Oakwood would
return. Put me out of this misery. I won't be sorry when
it's all over, I can tell you. (*Directly to audience.*) You, yes
you. The others might not have suspected. Or pretended
they didn't know, but I can no longer pretend. I have
been aware. From the outset. Of you. Looking at me.
Judging me. I don't know what you expected to see, but
I hope you are satisfied. There are some people who are
never satisfied unless they are watching other people
suffering. Other peoples' pain. I'm sorry, but isn't it
enough to be exposed in this manner, night after night,
not knowing what to say or what to do, or how to behave
without you, you always wanting more, some insight,
some revelation, some conclusion that gives you the
sense of security that there is, I don't know, some
answer? To give you the sense you understand. Well,
perhaps this is all there is. No deeper significance. I'm
sorry, I was forgetting the – what did John call them? –
the conventions of this situation in which I find
myself –

JOHN has entered.

JOHN: Mum.

STELLA: (*Startled.*) Who's there?

JOHN: It's me, Mum. I was looking for you.

STELLA: Well I was here. Here all the time.

JOHN: What were you doing, Mum?

STELLA: Talking.

JOHN: To who?

STELLA: To whom.

JOHN: To whom?

STELLA: To the walls. Who do you think?

JOHN: Perhaps it's for the better.

STELLA: I don't know what you mean.

JOHN: To…to let it out.

STELLA: To let what out? There is no 'it' to let out.

JOHN: Mum –

STELLA: I really don't have time for this.

JOHN: I'm leaving, Mum.

STELLA: You certainly pick your moments.

JOHN: You always said I should leave.

STELLA: Yes. Well. Now you are.

JOHN: Mum?

STELLA: What?

JOHN: What was her name, Mum?

STELLA: Whose name?

JOHN: The girl.

STELLA: What girl? When? There was no girl. I don't know what you mean. I never had a daughter. I would have liked to have...but I didn't...

JOHN: But Mum –

STELLA: I don't have time for this. Go if you're going. I have the sprouts to see to.

JOHN: ?

STELLA: The dinner. Tomorrow. O, where is that Man from Oakwood?

The MAN enters carrying toolbox, STELLA moves back upstage into the scene. JOHN remains downstage watching the action. No characters in this final scene appear to be aware of his presence apart from STELLA who watches him warily. The MAN retrieves any lost furniture as well as orchestrating the return of the walls.

MAN: There you are, Mrs Walls, I was looking for you. Sorry about the delay. Things were a little more complicated than I first thought. But I got the equipment, the new equipment. In fact, we're ready go with the first one.

STELLA: (*Helping to rearrange furniture.*) That is a relief. There's still so much to be done. I must say, I'd almost given up hope.

MAN: Didn't I tell you I'd sort you out? Here she comes –

STELLA: (*Panicked.*) Who?

MAN: The wall.

STELLA: (*Relieved.*) O yes. Yes, of course.

Kitchen wall descends. As soon as it touches the ground THEO enters from the kitchen pushing TOM. TOM is eating a Cadbury's Mini-Roll. There is a packet on his lap.

THEO: There you are Stella. We were looking for you.

TOM: Is it later, Walls?

THEO: A little, but not so you'd notice. He's a lot happier now, Stella. You're a lot happier now, aren't you Tom?

TOM: I was travelling, Walls. I was in the Zephyr. Travelling old hedgerowed country roads. And it was a hot day and the seat of my pants was stuck to my backside with the leather and the sweat. And I stopped by a field that was knee high with wild flowers and grasses and they kissed and tickled my legs. And I was young again and running. A boy. I saw the future and it was a summer's field. It was the happiness I was crying with, Walls, the happiness.

THEO: But you're alright now, father.

TOM: Where has my life gone? My world?

(Sings crackedly.) – *Star of the Sea.*
Pray for the wanderer, pray for me.

Timor mortis conturbat me, Walls, *timor mortis.* O God give me faith.

THEO: Lord graciously hear us. O by the way Stella, I had a rummage, and we did have some of those Cadbury's mini-rolls after all.

TOM: The Quakers. Aren't we all just God's little confectioners when it comes down to it.

THEO: I suppose we are, Tom, though I can't say I'd ever thought of it like that.

MAN: Second one's on it's way, Mrs Walls.

Back wall containing hall door descends. As it touches the ground SWEENEY enters through the hall door.

SWEENEY: There you all are. And Stella, we were looking for you. Just seeing the quack to his car. Says it's nothing to worry about. The turns. Way of all flesh, he says.

MAN: Third wall's all set, Mrs Walls.

THEO: Isn't he the great man? If I was still in underpants I'd find a place for a man like him.

SWEENEY: Bit of a tight squeeze, eh Walls?

Third wall descends. As it does so JOSEPH and MARY enter from the door that leads to hall, stairs and landing.

JOSEPH: There you all are. And Mum, we were looking –

STELLA: I was here. I was here all the time.

SWEENEY: And what were you two doing upstairs?

JOSEPH: Talking.

SWEENEY: Young people these days! There was no talking in our day I can tell you.

MARY: We were going to tell you later.

JOSEPH: But I suppose it is later now.

TOM: (*Panicked.*) Later? He said it's later, Walls –

THEO: Not so you'd notice, Tom, not so you'd notice.

SWEENEY: Well what were you going to tell us?

JOSEPH: Well myself and Mary, well Mary, actually –

SWEENEY: You're not?

JOSEPH: We are.

MARY: I am.

JOSEPH: She is.

SWEENEY: Well this calls for something. Joseph and Mary and their new baby at Christmas.

JOSEPH: If truth be told I'm not sure how…or when –

SWEENEY: He's not sure how! He's not sure how!

JOSEPH: I mean –

THEO: A photo. We should take a photo.

MAN: I've a camera. I'll take a photo for you. I like taking photos.

THEO: Isn't he the great man? Aren't we all great men? Even the women.

The MAN goes to his toolbox. He removes the framed photo he took earlier, places it back on the mantelpiece as if it were the most natural thing in the world. It is a different photo. This perhaps needs to be signified by a different frame. They all look at him as he does so. He finds his camera. THEO shepherds all the others, apart from JOHN, into a group portrait position. The conversation of all except STELLA becomes more distant.

THEO: Right, right, positions everyone.

STELLA: (*To JOHN.*) You still here?

THEO: We all here?

SWEENEY: Some more than others, Walls, some of us more than others.

THEO: The bould Sweeney. Always the life and soul.

STELLA: (*To JOHN.*) Well, what are you waiting for?

JOHN moves slowly towards hall door. The curtain, which is the exterior of a house proceeds to descend very slowly.

THEO: Stella you don't want to be over there, in the dark. Come back here Stella, into the light.

MARY: And look, the fourth wall. It's returning.

STELLA: (*To JOHN.*) What's keeping you? Go –

THEO: Everything back to normal.

MAN: Like I said, I do like a happy ending.

STELLA: (*To JOHN.*) See if I care. We'll carry on, don't you worry, carry on as if nothing happened. Carry on as if you'd never even been. A ghost. A ghost that's what you'll be. Go! Go on!

JOHN puts on his jacket and opens front door. The family regards their photographer.

MAN: Now everyone –

STELLA: (*To JOHN.*) Go on to hell for all I care!

MAN: Smile!

The MAN's camera flashes as JOHN slams the front door. The family freeze as the fourth wall continues its slow descent. Karen Carpenter sings 'Top of the World'.

The End.